HOW TO CREATE DIGITAL PORTFOLIOS TO APPLY FOR COLLEGE AND JOBS

NATALIE CHOMET

Rosen
YA™

New York

Published in 2018 by The Rosen Publishing Group, Inc.
29 East 21st Street, New York, NY 10010

Copyright © 2018 by The Rosen Publishing Group, Inc.

First Edition

Library of Congress Cataloging-in-Publication Data

Names: Chomet, Natalie, author.
Title: How to create digital portfolios to apply for college and jobs / Natalie Chomet.
Description: First edition. | New York, NY : Rosen Publishing, 2018. | Series: Project learning using digital portfolios | Includes bibliographical references and index.
Identifiers: LCCN 2017001513 | ISBN 9781508175285 (library bound book)
Subjects: LCSH: Electronic portfolios in education—Juvenile literature. | Employment portfolios—Juvenile literature.
Classification: LCC LB1029.P67 C46 2018 | DDC 650.14/2—dc23
LC record available at https://lccn.loc.gov/2017001513

Manufactured in China

CONTENTS

As teens, we all have a specific goal that we are striving to achieve. Whether it's getting into a dream school, getting that first real job, advancing your career, or transitioning into a new one, you're going to need something that will demonstrate your accomplishments, strengths, and interests. An application or a résumé is useful to give an outline of who you are as a student or professional. But even the most impressive résumé is at its most basic level a list of achievements, experiences, and skills.

How do you separate yourself from the pile of other applicants? When crafting a story, to make the writing the most powerful, a skilled author will often employ the following principle: show, don't tell. For example, it's more exciting to write a passage describing the sound of a bat hitting a baseball and the sound of the roaring crowd in the batter's ears as he runs around the bases than to simply state that the player made a home run. This strategy can be applied to your professional life as well. A portfolio of your best work will show your future school or employer the quality of work you are capable of much better than an application alone can.

From writing to visual arts, scientific research, politics, or coding, having strong examples of your work will only serve to make you a stronger candidate. Before websites were ubiquitous, people put together a portfolio of physical copies of their work. For example, if someone was interviewing for a graphic design position at an ad agency, the applicant would bring a portfolio of examples of the best designs she had made to show both quality and range of work. ("Show, don't

It's important to be prepared for your interview. A very simple way to arm yourself for an upcoming interview is by printing copies of your résumé, cover letter, and writing samples, if applicable.

tell" in action!) The interviewer would notice right away the qualities that set that person apart. Perhaps it would be a unique style, extreme attention to detail, or a versatility shown through diverse examples. Whatever it was, it would show the uniqueness of the person much more effectively.

A digital portfolio serves the same purpose as a traditional physical one, but technology has improved upon the original model. Though the goal is the same—show one's personality and high level and breadth of work—there are more ways to organize, present, and update a digital portfolio. It's easy to share and update a portfolio when it is online. No need to lug a folder full of papers around any more. All it takes is a quick email or a link in your LinkedIn profile to show people your portfolio. If you made it when you were a high school sophomore and you want to update it with your junior year extracurricular activities and SAT scores, you don't have to start from scratch. A well thought-out design—using hyperlinks, separate web pages, a menu bar across the top, and more—can make a large quantity of information more easily discoverable. Whether you know HTML or not, there are plenty of ways to make your digital portfolio look sleek, professional, and one of a kind. It's a surefire way to make your future school or employer see you that way, too.

CHAPTER ONE

WHAT IS A DIGITAL PORTFOLIO?

S till not entirely sure what a digital portfolio is? Think about the function of a portfolio: as a student, it shows the learning, achievements, and scholastic and extracurricular interests of the student to prospective colleges and even current teachers; as a professional, it demonstrates the accomplishments, range of work, and specialties to potential employers.

A physical portfolio can accomplish this, of course, but using digital tools can have more advantages. Using multimedia features allows the creator to demonstrate aptitude and skill with not only

What could be more convenient than a portfolio that fits in the palm of your hand? Digital tools make your work more portable and easier to store and distribute.

text, but also sound, graphics, illustration, and video. If computer skills are your forte, you can embed your expertise within the very format of the portfolio itself. It's easy to showcase a musical composition, performance, oral presentation, and self-reflections and assessments in this format. An added benefit of hosting the portfolio online is how easy it is to update your work, adding more recent and even more sophisticated examples as you grow as a student and professional.

WHAT'S IN A (TRADITIONAL) PORTFOLIO?

In order to figure out what to put in your digital portfolio, you should consider what a traditional, physical portfolio would hold.

In a professional-looking container, a carefully organized sampling of your work would be held. If you were an artist, you would want to include a few realistic pictures, such as a still life, a few impressionistic examples, modern nonrepresentational works, and perhaps a few different media such as oil paintings, pastels, charcoals, watercolors, and even photographs or pictures of statues. The same range would apply no matter what your professional focus. If you were a writer, short stories, nonfiction, persuasive essays, and research papers on authors or specific works would demonstrate talent and experience in diverse styles. If you work in the nonprofit sector, you could provide examples of all the different types of events and fund-raising efforts you have taken part in: walks and races, bake sales, concerts or performances, and telethons, as well as examples of how these fund-raisers were advertised.

Your digital portfolio should follow the same general principles. Design it in a way that is both pleasing to the eye and professional. It should be organized so that you can easily find each piece, and the pieces should be grouped thematically by style. A few examples within each style should be displayed. If you have one specific focus, such as journalistic photography, you can have the majority of your examples be in this style.

Your portfolio should reflect your personality and interests. Make a list of goals and things you're passionate about to help give your portfolio focus.

ADVANTAGES OF A DIGITAL FORMAT

Hosting your portfolio online enables you to be creative in both the presentation and organization of the information you choose to include. Do you want to have a main page with links to separate categories of work? This could be an ideal format for a student to show all the different subjects in which he excels. A homepage with an "About Me" section would give an overview of the student's interests and goals. A menu across the top of the page could link to different pages of the student's strongest examples of his work: creative writing samples, research papers on social studies topics, a video of a debate, a chorus recital, a collection of lab reports, and science fair projects.

Will each page have a header image? For artists or photographers, these images could be their own graphics, drawings, or photographs. You could even include animations that you've made, if that's a skill

If you're an artist, you can include your illustrations within the design of your digital portfolio. Get creative and have fun with it!

you want to demonstrate. This could also be a good opportunity for travel enthusiasts or Fulbright scholars to display the different places they have visited.

The small details you add to your portfolio can show your personality as well as your attention to detail. Will you include links allowing the reader to "jump down" to a particular section on the page? The font and color scheme can be selected from templates or based on your own eye for aesthetics. You could outfit the header of your portfolio with a logo design of your name. There are many possibilities. As long as you host it on a template or website that is easy for you to use, the power is at your fingertips.

A digital portfolio doesn't just show who you are as a student and professional, it also tells the viewer that you have the awareness and maturity to self-reflect. It isn't easy to represent oneself in an organized and well-rounded way. To select the cream-of-the-crop examples of your work shows that you can self-edit. Also, not picking too few examples gives the viewer a full idea of who you are, as does not presenting too many samples to wade through.

WHEN'S THE RIGHT TIME TO BEGIN?

When's a good time to start your digital portfolio? Chances are the time is now. You may start it your sophomore year and then by junior year have even more examples to display in your portfolio or a specific concentration you'd like to showcase to prospective colleges. Better to start early and update often so that by the time you're ready to show it to admissions offices, it has been edited and refined to include the best examples of your work. If you want to major in history, your relevant PSAT score and your best history research paper can be your featured samples. If chemistry is your passion, test scores and science fair experiments may be the main event. You could even write your name across the top using the periodic table as your canvas!

When you start high school you may not have a clear idea of what you want to major in when you get to college or even what types of colleges you'd like to apply to. In any case, you can still start your portfolio and be ahead of the game when the time comes to choose a major. Start with the best three examples of your work from each subject, from English to math class. There's always time to get specific later. Add to that all the community service and activities outside of academics that you do, such as the track team, bands, clubs, and service organizations such as Arista, Boy Scouts of America, or even volunteering in a soup kitchen each Thanksgiving. Then, you'll have a great foundation to base your portfolio on.

Volunteering activities are a great way to show that you make time for things that are important to you and that you give back to your community.

Let's say you go on a few college tours the beginning of your junior year and decide you'd like to go to a certain type of school or focus on a specific subject. You can take the examples you started with and narrow them down based on the concentration you've decided on. You'll still give the overall impression of being a well-rounded and multifaceted student, but you can make sure the majority of your examples are within your area of focus.

The same general approach applies to your professional portfolio. It may be that when you graduate college, you don't have as specific a professional focus as after a few years of working. Depending on how much experience you have, it will determine where your examples come from. When you graduate and are looking for your first full-time job, your portfolio may contain a mix of relevant schoolwork as well as a few internships and summer jobs. Once you've entered the workforce for a few years, you may deem it appropriate to retire the majority of these examples. It's good to be able to weed out your portfolio periodically with an eye for the impression you give to outsiders. If you keep your internships and part-time and summer work in your portfolio while you have significant professional experience, you may accidentally give the impression that you are less experienced than you in fact are. Sometimes less is more.

CHAPTER TWO

TOOLS AND TECHNIQUES: BUILDING YOUR DIGITAL PORTFOLIO

Once you have a clear idea of what a digital portfolio is and how you can benefit from having one, the natural next step is building one. Technically speaking, a digital portfolio is a website that focuses on you and your professional or academic achievements. The structure and content of the website itself is what makes it a portfolio. Once you get a handle on the basic mechanics needed to create your digital portfolio, you can focus on refining it, both in its format and its content.

STEP ONE: WHERE DOES IT LIVE?

Before you can begin making a digital portfolio, you need to determine where it will live. You'll need to figure out where to host your website. Some website-building resources will host your site for you. It may, however, be worth your while to purchase your own domain name. A custom domain name can be purchased from various companies and costs less than $10 a year

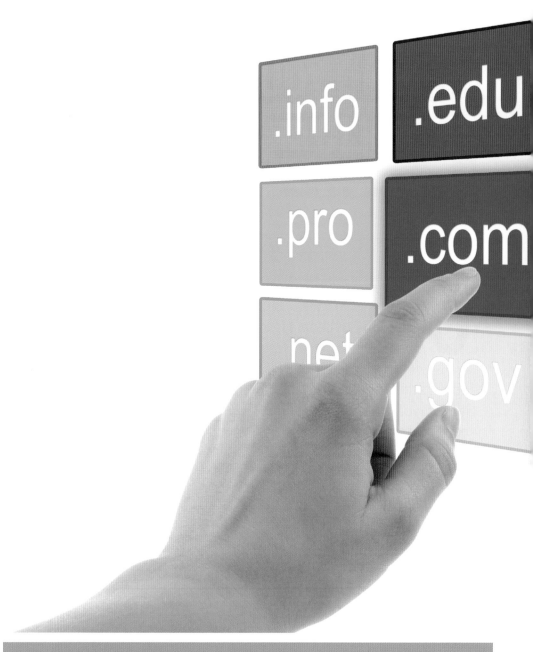

Choosing a URL may be more important than you think. Keep in mind that you want every facet of your digital portfolio to give a professional impression.

depending on which company you choose. Potential employers can easily discover your website if you purchase a domain name.

Make sure to choose wisely. Use some iteration of your name that sounds professional and catchy. Also, make sure no one has the rights to that domain. Your domain name can be straightforward, creative, or practical. Your digital portfolio will be perceived more seriously if the domain on which it is hosted echoes your name. You may have a stronger impact on a college administrator or future employer this way, as opposed to your name appearing at the end of a long URL after a slash or period.

STEP TWO: HOW TO BUILD IT

Once you determine where you're hosting your digital portfolio, you'll want to figure out how you'll build it. You have many options depending

WEBSITE PLATFORM EXAMPLES

Purchase a custom domain.
- **Domains.google**
- **DomainsMadeSimple.com**
- **GoDaddy.com**
- **Register.com**
- **Register.hostgator.com**

Build a digital portfolio.
Journalism/media, English, writing, public relations, communications:
- **Clippings.me. Add your best clippings, or samples of your writing, and customize the look and feel without any coding necessary.**
- **Pressfolios. Keep track of your stories, organize them, and present them in an attractive format.**

Art, design, and other creative interests:
- **Behance. Showcase and broadcast your creative work with sleek templates.**
- **Carbonmade. This manageable tool showcases creative design portfolios.**
- **Crevado. Free and easy-to-use site to host your creative works on beautifully designed templates.**

General resources that will fit the bill, regardless of your area of interest:
- **Seelio. Helps students create online portfolios to tell their professional story.**

- **Squarespace. Intuitive platform to build clean, modern-looking websites.**
- **VisualCV. Easy tool to create résumés, personal landing pages, and online portfolios.**
- **Wix. Free website-building tool that does not require coding.**
- **Wordpress. Create your own blog or personal website for free.**

on your comfort level with web design, how hands-on you want to be, and what type of portfolio you are creating. There are several reliable free resources for creating your digital portfolio. You'll want to take care that the one you choose is appropriate to your industry or academic concentration. There are also resources that will fit any career or educational interest. You may choose to build your portfolio on a personal website-building platform.

STEP THREE: GET TECHNICAL WITH IT: CODE ON YOUR OWN

Are you a coding whiz? Whether this is a professional passion or personal hobby, using your knowledge of code to create your digital portfolio will not only allow you to have complete and total control over the look and feel of your site, it will also be a professional asset. Knowledge of code is a big advantage to many career

If you're versed in coding, demonstrate your skill by embedding your own code into the design of your digital portfolio.

paths, and most potential employers and colleges, if it isn't already your professional focus, will view it as a perk. It's skills such as these that will set you apart. And being able to showcase those skills in the very fabric of your portfolio is a seamless and direct selling tool, especially when you have a great-looking site to show for it.

Whether you know how to build a website from scratch or not, it may make the most sense to use a content management system (CMS) to get started. That way, the complex tools are already baked in and it will save you time and maybe even a headache or two later on.

You can also include your customized website theme or template in your portfolio. That's an effective way to show off

EXPERT ADVICE

Here's some advice direct from corporate human resources. To get a digital portfolio that "pops," follow a few key rules of thumb:

- Pick your strongest samples of work. Try to find between seven and ten examples. (Supposedly eight is the magic number.) They should demonstrate your main strengths and be current—no older than five years. In order, lead with your strongest and end with a close second. You want to start and end on a high note.
- Clearly categorize your work. Be organized. Whether that means working chronologically or by type of work, be sure there's a method to the madness. The format may be best determined depending on your industry.
- Show your creativity. Let potential employers or colleges get a sense of who you are. Target your audience. Always keep in mind who will be reading it and what they would want to see, but through consistency of your presentation and the examples you include, your portfolio can and should show your personality.

your coding skills and eye for design. If you're a designer, coder, or freelancer, it'll be an easy way to fill up your portfolio fast. Showing off a website that you have built from beginning to end is its own advertisement. You may end up getting requests to build websites for other people. Showing what you can build is the quickest and most descriptive way to demonstrate your skills. There should be more than a paragraph or two of text explaining what you do.

STEP FOUR: FORM AND FUNCTION

Whether you've picked a website with a selection of templates or you've opted to build your portfolio using your knowledge of code, you need to determine what the design of your digital portfolio will look like. What are the most important aspects of a good design? The structure of your portfolio should have logic to it: organized, easily navigable information laid out in a

Including your hobbies is a great way to give your portfolio personality. Whether it's photography or travel, finding a way to weave in your passions will give it unique flavor.

way that the most important items are readily visible and simple enough that you can update it periodically. It would be a shame to spend time and energy putting together a digital portfolio, only to have it become outdated after a year or two. The design you decide upon should not be difficult to go back into to make changes.

How do you determine how your portfolio will be laid out? If you're using a website that provides templates, look through them and see if there's a format that will organize your information the best. You can come up with a format in the same way that you start a paper: make an outline. Be clear about what information you'll include and rate how important each piece is. Try to approach it as an outsider would. If someone didn't know anything about you, what would be the first thing you'd want him or her to learn? And after that, what samples best exemplify your work? Last, what is the overall impression you hope to leave the reader with?

Another practical way to get an idea of how you want to structure your portfolio is to work off a model. Perhaps you know a few people in your field of interest who have digital portfolios you can look at for reference. You can ask a counselor or a career adviser if they have samples they can share. Many colleges as well as other educational websites have a few student digital portfolios in various fields that you can look up online as well. It can be a waste of time to reinvent the wheel, especially when there are people who have gone through this before. Perhaps they've already made the mistakes that you are bound to make. They have gone through this process and refined their portfolios the long way. Better to learn by strong example and make your digital portfolio as solid and impressive as it can be.

CHAPTER THREE

INTRODUCING YOU: WHAT GOES INTO YOUR PORTFOLIO?

The structure and organization of your portfolio is important. In order to determine that, you'll need to decide what you plan to include in it. Come up with a list of items then rank them in order of importance and quality. You'll want to narrow it down so that you have only the strongest examples of your work but include enough to give the reader an idea of your style and range.

A digital portfolio is a website with a specific purpose: to show who you are as a professional and what your aspirations are. Beginning with the homepage, each section should tell a different and integral piece of

If you get stuck, a career adviser or professional in your field of interest can give you expert advice. Don't be afraid to ask for help!

GETTING STARTED

Below is a list of questions to ask yourself that will help you jump-start your portfolio:

- **Who is your audience?**
- **What are the things that you are passionate about?**
- **What are your top goals for the next year or even five years?**
- **Distill your pitch to a tweet-length phrase (about 125 characters). What do you have to offer? Use ten words or less.**
- **What three to four words would you use to describe your personality?**
- **What are your strongest skills? Not just according to you, but also to friends, family, coworkers, or peers?**

your story. If you structure it well, and make your selections with care, your digital portfolio should tell a compelling and unique story: who you are. And it will be a story that your target audience—whether a potential employer or your dream-college admissions officer—will want to read from beginning to end.

THE HOMEPAGE

First things first: create your homepage. This is the first thing anyone who visits your digital portfolio will see. What do you want it to look like? You could include a cover photo that you have taken. Or you could opt to use a graphic you have designed, perhaps of your name, like on a résumé. What type of information will you include on this page? Here are a few tips to keep in mind:

- **Keep It Simple.** You want it to look clean and uncluttered.
- **Basic Relevant Information.** You should include your name, school, and major. If you have graduated more than five years ago, this information may not need to be as prominent. Although it is still relevant and important, you should find somewhere on the page to include it.
- **An Introduction.** A few sentences stating your passions, experience, and the skills that will make you an ideal candidate. Think of this as your mission statement to your employers or prospective colleges.
- **Navigation.** Depending on how your portfolio is laid out, it may be helpful to mention how to navigate to find more information. ("You can find my résumé and recent work...") This section may not be necessary for every layout. You may opt instead to have a menu of contents across the top or along the left-hand side of the page.

WHAT ABOUT ME?

You will want to include either on the main page or linked clearly from the homepage an "About Me" section. Imagine that your future employer or college is reading this section; decide what you

If you're not sure how to get started on your "About Me" section, pretend you're having a conversation with someone you just met.

want them to know about you. You can start with basics: where you're from, your school, major/minor or professional focus, any relevant work or internships and briefly what it was you did, extra-curricular activities or clubs, contact information, and any other information you may deem important to share. You may want to include a current photo of you on this page as well.

This is the prime opportunity for you to display your personality. You

DO'S AND DON'TS

DON'T include an awkward profile picture.
DO feature a recent photo of yourself smiling, looking straight forward, with good lighting and professional attire.

DON'T make visitors hunt for your work or show small replicas of your samples.
DO make your work organized, very easy to view, and easily discoverable from your homepage.

DON'T clutter your digital portfolio with too much information, from copy to graphic elements, or even too many samples of work.
DO keep the layout of your portfolio simple, clean, and easy to browse. Choose your samples with care, displaying the strongest examples of your work.

DON'T direct potential employers or college administrators to any social media pages that contain personal discussions or content.
DO maintain a social media presence that is professional. Link to this one in your portfolio, and have your social media link back to these channels.

DON'T shy away from expressing who you are, what your passions are, and how you approach your work. **DO** include a brief explanation of each work, as well as a description of who you are and what your goals are. Let the viewer learn who you are through your interests, skills, and experience.

can convey it in your tone of writing. Though the style should obviously be professional, perhaps you have a sense of humor or a descriptive and colorful way of writing. It should be your voice. The details you opt to share in this section can also say a lot about you as a person. Do you have the travel bug, feel passionate about serving your community, or love to express yourself creatively? The examples of work and activities you include in this section will tell that story. Even your photo can say something important about you. It could be in your hometown or a place where you traveled to study, or it could show an activity you love. Every piece of information in your digital portfolio is a chance to tell your story.

SHOW AND TELL—EMPHASIS ON SHOW

Once you've planned out your homepage and your "About Me" section, it's time to put together the meat of your portfolio. Be sure that your schooling and professional experience is listed somewhere that makes organizational sense on your digital portfolio. If you have won awards or earned scholarships, these

Showing a wide array of work samples will demonstrate how versatile and well-rounded you are. Whether you take panoramic photos of vistas, make short videos, or have a cooking blog, samples of your work will show your many facets.

should be displayed in a logical place as well. Now the next step is to include relevant examples of your work.

Keeping in mind your audience at all times is key. What is your objective? Whether it's a career in advertising or animation, you'll want to provide examples of your work that demonstrate a high quality, as well as show the types of work that you hope to do at your dream job. Showing a wide array of examples that demonstrate different styles or skills you have is a great strategy as well. Employers want to see that you have a range as well as flexibility. The ability to be flexible is a quality that can be applied to any career. It's an asset to be able to do good work, no matter the style that's required. Showing a variety of examples also covers

When deciding which writing samples to include, asking the basic question, "What purpose does this piece serve?" will help you make your selections.

your bases. You never can tell what will strike the fancy of a college administrator or a potential employer. If you have several samples that cover different styles, you'll have a greater chance of appealing to viewers—no matter what their background may be.

Narrow down your examples using your best judgment. If you're not sure if you should include something, ask yourself a few questions:

- Is this demonstrating a skill or style that my other examples do not?
- Is this a sample I am especially proud of?
- Is this a style I hope to do more of in my future career or study at school?

- What is unique about it, or what does it accomplish that my other samples do not?

The answers to these questions will likely crystallize whether a piece is truly adding something to your portfolio or if it is just more of the same. Once you select and organize your samples, it's time to show your portfolio to a few people. Share it with your parents, a peer in your industry, or a guidance counselor or teacher you admire. These people will come with an outside perspective and may have constructive critiques to offer. It's also good to have a few people read it besides yourself. It always takes a few extra pairs of eyes to catch any spelling or grammatical mistakes. You'll want to eliminate any of those errors before sharing it with your intended audience. You don't want any minor mistakes detracting from the overall effect of your portfolio.

CHAPTER FOUR

DIGITAL PORTFOLIOS FOR APPLYING TO COLLEGE

Applying to colleges can be a daunting process. High school students prepare themselves by taking AP courses, joining after-school clubs, volunteering, and keeping their grades and test scores up. This is standard practice for being a good student and impressive college candidate. If you were to list your accomplishments on paper, what would make this list stand out from the others? A typical college application may appear to be a series of lists and items to check off—from transcripts, to essays, recommendations, and SAT scores—however, in order to put together a unique

If you forget about AP classes, grades, and test scores for a moment, what else makes you stand out?

and successful college application, you'll need to read between the lines and provide something more cohesive than all these disparate items. What do all these lists and items achieve as a whole? They describe you as a student. Therefore, in order to make your application as strong and compelling as it can be and as unique as your personality, it has to tell your story.

A great way to tell your story is by going beyond the simple questions, answers, and lists that are required of all applicants. Create a digital portfolio, and you'll have the perfect medium through which to communicate who you are as a student, person, and young professional.

Everyone's story is going to be different—that's the point. The types of information as well as the format will depend on what you are interested in and what your strengths are. Each college applicant can't be reduced to a category—much less merely four of them. The following profiles are meant to be examples from which most people will hopefully find a few nuggets of information that they can apply to themselves.

THE ATHLETICALLY GIFTED

The design of your digital portfolio can and should reflect its main focus, or theme. If the goal is to get a scholarship to a school with a stellar track team, you can work this thread through different aspects of your portfolio. You can include photos from races as header images. Perhaps the background of the main page is one big track field. Track could be the metaphor for success that gives your "About Me" section shape.

Include races won, the teams you've been on, and the work you've put in to achieve your goal. You may even eventually want to include a testimonial or recommendation from a coach. But also think from your audience's perspective; know that they

ADVICE FROM AN INSIDER

Though no two portfolios should be the same, college admissions officers want to see certain elements in them to determine their effectiveness. Here are a few that come directly from the source:

- **Metacognition:** Show that you can reflect on your work and think about your progress and what you learned along the way. This shows that as a student, you have an understanding of your own academic journey. Demonstrate that you found meaning from your experiences and learned from things you've tried.

- **Connected learning:** Show that you have made connections between things you have learned—across classes and extracurricular experiences. For example, a volunteering experience could teach you leadership qualities that you then applied to a group project in the classroom. More broadly, the connections between all the projects you do (or samples you show in your portfolio) can demonstrate what you want to do as a professional or the type of learner you are.

- **Personality:** Let's say your interest is biology. Your digital portfolio may be impressive and well organized, but showing your experiments, projects, and test scores is not enough to show who you are as a person. A hobby like drawing or photography can be easily incorporated to show your artistic side. Or including hobbies and passions in your "About Me" section can flesh out your personality to the reader.

will want to see that you are more than a devoted member of the track team, even if you're its star. Include your other interests, whether it's a passion for the history of WWII or a penchant for picking up foreign languages. Find a way to let the other facets of your personality come through.

THE ARTISTICALLY INCLINED

If you're an artist looking to go to school to finely hone your craft, chances are you already know you should include a portfolio of your best work as part of your submission. When choosing the pieces you will include, don't simply look for your strongest work. Perhaps in choosing those pieces, you should take a look

If you already know what you want to focus on, go to your dream school's website and look up the required courses for this major. Looking this up will help you decide which art pieces to include.

at the syllabus of your top-choice school. Determine from the list the classes you would most like to take. This should give you a concrete place to start. If there are specific requirements for your major, those will be classes that you'll want to demonstrate an aptitude for. Now you'll be sure to select a range of work, and each piece will serve its own purpose.

You'll demonstrate your depth of knowledge and range of ability with your samples, but the portfolio itself can also be your canvas. If coding and graphic design are not your strengths, pick a template that suits your purposes. You can select images (maybe your own) and a color scheme that make your portfolio stand out with both its form and content.

THE STEM FOCUSED

Whether you won the Intel scholarship or your school's science fair, a STEM-focused college applicant can find positive examples of his or her methodical mind. Perhaps something that sets you apart is the choice to include an example of an experiment that did not work out as you planned. This shows a perceptiveness and realistic nature that not all budding scientists have. Most experiments don't work out the first, second, or third time around. As long as you show that you learned something from the process, you will also reveal something positive and resilient about yourself.

Though science, technology, math, or engineering is your passion, you must show that you have other interests and personality traits. Your "About Me" can reveal part of your personality that wouldn't be apparent in your samples of work. Perhaps you have an anecdote about your scientific mind as a child. You may want to include a hobby or extracurricular activity such as playing an instrument or a passion for cooking (maybe

From singing in the school play to hosting your own podcast, your hobbies can make you a more three-dimensional candidate.

this ties into your passion for chemistry, too). Whatever you include, remember that admissions wants to get to know you as a whole person.

THE RENAISSANCE STUDENT

A good student who has varied interests academically and even outside of school has many strengths. You don't have to be sure what you want to major in to make a great impression on colleges. Exploring different courses to see where your passions take you is part of what college is about. You have your work cut out for you. You have activities (plays, volunteering, creative writing, or maybe a podcast) and classes in which you excel. You may have won a contest or a scholarship in the past few years. These aspects of your profile as a student are important, but that doesn't mean you can throw the kitchen sink into your digital portfolio.

Organization is key. Separate your high school experience into categories. This will help determine what is necessary to show a part of your personality and what you may not need. It is possible that certain categories or samples within them will not make the cut. A simple way to start putting everything in place is to separate school from extracurricular. Maybe awards and recommendations will have their own section, while performances, artwork, or writing samples can have another. When you're done, you should have a portfolio that is as well rounded as you are. Your menu itself will tell a story.

CHAPTER FIVE

DIGITAL PORTFOLIOS FOR GETTING A JOB

Digital portfolios aren't only useful for getting into college. While in school, during the summer, or after you graduate, there will be times you'll want to be able to demonstrate your abilities and interests to a prospective employer. Your digital portfolio, whether you created one to get into college or now, can be an effective tool to communicate what you have to offer. No matter what job you want, there are certain aspects of the job-seeking process that will remain the same: finding the right opportunities for you, making connections between your skill sets and those required for the positions to

Interviews are the place where you can really show your personality and passion for a position, but your digital portfolio can help get you through the door!

which you apply, and laying a strong groundwork for the overlap between what the hiring managers want to see and what you have to offer.

Finding those positions will help drive what you want your portfolio to look like. Not that you would misrepresent any qualities and experience you have, but there will be aspects that you'll want to emphasize depending on the opportunities you are looking at. That's why it is so important to think like the hiring managers you want to appeal and stand out to. Do your research when applying for a job and preparing your digital portfolio. Always ask yourself what the person doing the hiring would want to see in an applicant.

THE SCIENTIST

If you're looking for a career in the sciences, your digital portfolio will have to satisfy some specific requirements. You will want to show your main focus and the projects and/or experiments you have worked on, but you will want to do more than a résumé or cover letter could accomplish alone. Ask yourself: What's unique about me that makes me interesting, or an asset even?

Here's an example of how your portfolio could generally be organized: Lead with your "About Me" section, which should include details to give a sense of your background and interests, science-related and beyond. Your résumé or CV should appear as well, to detail your experience. You can break it into sections if necessary, organizing the information and breaking it up visually (example: professional experience, education, awards, leadership, conferences, etc.). The clear advantage of a digital resource is having more space to fully flesh out the impressive work you've done. That's why you'll want to include a section of projects or experiments to show the work you've dedicated

ADVICE FROM THE OTHER SIDE OF THE HIRING DESK

What do prospective employers want to see when they are hiring? What's your pitch? This should succinctly describe what your personal and professional goals are. This is what you want your employer to see in your "About Me" section. In crafting your personal pitch, always consider the needs of your target audience. What solution are you providing for the company?

What don't hiring managers want to see in your profile? Information that may be considered personal and not relevant to your work life and persona as an employee should be eliminated from your digital portfolio. Do link to your LinkedIn profile, but perhaps skip linking your Twitter or Facebook pages if they are more personal than professional. Also refrain from sharing personal details (marital status, etc.) on LinkedIn. LinkedIn is considered a professional network, and the details you share on your profile are more likely to be germane to the jobs you want to get.

It's possible that you have curated a social media persona that is professional as well. Perhaps you have a blog discussing matters that are relevant to your industry. You may share your articles across other social media channels. Twitter is often used to discuss professional topics as well as share articles written by others on such topics. If you have taken the time and care to maintain a professional (and professionally relevant) social media presence, by all means share it in your portfolio. If you use these channels for social purposes (photos of friends, etc.) that's fine. This isn't something you'd need to hide— it's just not something that will be necessary to highlight in this particular forum.

Reference your LinkedIn profile in your digital portfolio and vice versa. It is a helpful way to share your experience with your professional network.

to your field and the innovative ideas you have. This section can include visual elements such as infographics and graphs to illustrate your work.

THE COMMUNICATOR

If you have a degree in communications, there are many directions your major can take you professionally. You will want to tailor your digital portfolio according to your specific career goals. Your "About Me" section can include insight into your background, such as where you grew up. For a personal yet professional touch, you could include a slideshow of photos captioned with each of the conferences, projects, and jobs/internships at which they were taken. This will both put a face to a name and illustrate your experience. Personal touches like this will help set you apart. Your résumé should be easily visible and include the information most pertinent to the career you want. Additionally, you will want to include a section that goes into more detail about your experience. You can decide what you want to call it—projects, campaigns, portfolio, etc. There you will go into detail about the projects you worked on. Show visuals when you can to illustrate social media, email campaigns, and presentations you have worked on.

THE DESIGNER

In a design portfolio, form is nearly as important as function. You'll want to show your aesthetic and skill as an artist. It would be shortsighted to let this show in your samples alone. Your style should come through clearly in every section. First, determine what kinds of jobs you want. You may want to research the aesthetics of the companies you admire most. You can use your portfolio to demonstrate what a good fit you are and even get some pointers from the look and feel of these companies' websites. Ask yourself: What is my signature? If you're a photographer, your crisp images can slide across the screen. If animation is your forte, an undulating animation could be your splash page. Perhaps you have a penchant for pop art. You could let that show through in the buttons, background, and colors of each page. Let your personality shine through and your portfolio will be like no other. Just be sure that—as lovely as it looks—your site has the easy functionality and legibility it needs to succeed. Don't let the design make the content hard to decipher.

Even if you're artistically inclined, it is important to make sure you don't let the design of your portfolio hinder its usefulness or legibility in any way.

THE TRAVELER

Whether you majored in international studies, foreign languages, or art history, your passion is traveling to faraway places. Let your career goals dictate the details you most want to feature, but your travel bug should add fun and personal flair to your digital portfolio. You have many options for the information you will want to include. You can illustrate your portfolio with photos of places you have visited. In addition to your "About Me" and résumé, include details that ground you as a professional. Perhaps this means adding a section of service experience (volunteering, tutoring, committees, and more). You may want to include a selection of papers you have written. If you studied or did a scholarship abroad, you could include a section that goes into detail about your experience in that country. You could even include a slideshow of images you captured while you were there. If you kept a blog while on your travels, this may be a great touch to show your skill as a travel writer/blogger. You have a lot of options for what to include and a great forum to show your passion and personality with professionalism.

CHAPTER SIX

SETTING YOURSELF APART

W hether you have created a digital portfolio to share with colleges or future employers, it is important to remember that it isn't a static thing. Whenever you began working on it, you will have new accomplishments and experiences that will be important to share. In order to keep it up to date, you may want to come up with a schedule for when you will add updates periodically, rather than leave it up to chance that you will remember. If you're in school, take a moment at the end of each semester to make changes. If you're working, do it every six months or quarterly. You can set a reminder in your calendar if that works best for you.

WHAT SHOULD YOU UPDATE?

When you sit down at the appointed time to make your updates, what will they be? Think about your end goal and take a moment to reflect on the past few months. What have you done that you are the most proud of? Have there been any events such as conferences or performances that should be documented? Chances are, once you stop and think about it, there will be at least a few aspects of your academic or professional life that are worthy of note. As always, keep your audience in mind and ask yourself, if you were on the other side of the hiring or admissions process, what would you want to see?

Updating your digital portfolio isn't only about making additions. Make it part of your updating process to look through each section and clean it up. This may entail a few tweaks to your "About Me" section. There may be a few details that you will want to add and a few that no longer seem necessary to emphasize. You may also want to make changes to your résumé and list of activities. As time goes on, things you did earlier in your academic or professional career may seem less important or even juvenile. Once you have had a few years of

As you progress in your career and gain more professional experience, certain details in your portfolio, such as college extracurricular activities, may become less relevant.

experience working in your field of expertise, you may not need to include your summer internships while you were in college. It's good to take these moments every so often so that you can reflect on the overall arc of your accomplishments. Doing so will mean that each update will be fairly quick and painless, more so than if you let it go for too long. Your digital portfolio isn't a paper résumé; it is a live document that people besides you likely have access to. You never know when someone may look you up. What would you like them to find?

MAINTAINING YOUR ONLINE PRESENCE

If a future employer or college admissions office looks you up online, they will find more than your digital portfolio. In order to maintain a mature, professional online presence, you will have to manage more than your digital portfolio. This includes social media channels such as Facebook, Twitter, and Instagram, as well as if you have a blog or write for any websites professionally or recreationally. This is not to say you should completely censor yourself. Just be judicious about what you share, and be aware of your privacy settings. If you have to think twice about sharing something online, perhaps it isn't worth the risk.

If a future employer searched on the internet for you, what would they find? This is the ultimate test of what an employer might find. If you take these steps every so often, you'll be ensuring you are in control of your image and you'll know exactly what they'll see.

Search for your name on the internet and see what comes up. If something is associated with your name in error, you can report it to Google and they may be able to take it down. This is

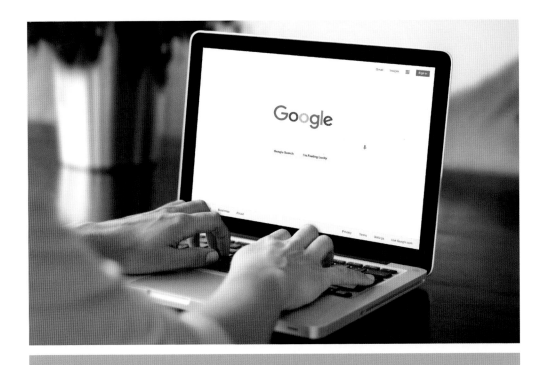

Have you Googled yourself lately? See what you can find about yourself.

also a good trick to see what comes up from your social media. It may not be as private as you think!

Click the button under privacy settings on your Facebook profile that allows you to view your profile as someone else. Try viewing it as someone who isn't friends with you. If you're not happy with what remains visible, you can change your settings overall or even on each individual post. Check back in on this anytime Facebook updates. Sometimes things appear more public after an update, as your settings may have changed. Keep in mind that your profile picture is visible to everyone, so keep it work-friendly.

BREAK FREE OF THE COOKIE CUTTER

A vital point to keep in mind is representing yourself as an individual. Your digital portfolio should be as unique as you are. If you include choice personal touches, you will paint an accurate portrait of yourself and therefore set yourself apart. What kinds of details show your personality, beyond your work and school experience?

- Special skills. Languages you know, coding skills, or any special certifications.
- Special interests/hobbies. Your travels, volunteer work, community activism, or school performances.
- Personal touches. Photos/drawings you've done, pictures of you, details about your upbringing, and things that have influenced you.

These little details will shed light on what you're passionate about and what motivates you to strive for your goals.

DIGITAL PORTFOLIOS THAT GO BEYOND

Just because you got into your dream school or you scored your first job, it doesn't mean you'll never need your digital portfolio again. Keep updating it because it may come in handy in the future. Let's say you've been working at your job for some time, and you'd like to ask for a raise or promotion. Your digital portfolio may come in handy since it can make your case, showing your accomplishments in a clear, professional format.

If you've been in a career path that you aren't excited about anymore, or perhaps you haven't exactly broken into the field that was your goal at the outset, you can use your digital portfolio to emphasize the aspects of your experience that apply to the job you do want. Perhaps the unconventional path will endow you with special skills that others who took the traditional path may not have to offer.

The time you put into your digital portfolio isn't simply a one-time benefit. Taking the time to build it from the ground up will save you effort

Update your portfolio once a year at least, so that it doesn't become obsolete. You can set a date in your calendar each year as a helpful reminder.

later on, making it easier to keep it updated. It serves a purpose beyond applying to jobs and colleges. It offers the opportunity to reflect on your achievements. This metacognition will serve you well in the long term, keeping you focused on what you want to get out of your career today, tomorrow, and for years to come.

GLOSSARY

aesthetic A particular artistic or visual style that defines how something looks.

coding Writing in any of several computer languages to translate what you want a program or website to do or look like.

content management system (CMS) A software application or set of programs that are used to create and manage digital content.

curate To select, organize, and present online content using professional expertise.

CV (curriculum vitae) A brief account of one's education, qualifications, and past experience.

discoverability The quality of being easy to find using a search engine or within a well-designed website.

diverse Showing a good amount of variety.

domain A web address or set of addresses that are all under the control of a specific organization or individual.

hosting Storing a website or other data on a server so that it can be accessed on the internet.

HTML (hypertext markup language) A standardized language for tagging text files so that they have font, color, graphic, and hyperlink effects on web pages.

hyperlink A link to another location or file that is activated by clicking on a highlighted word or image.

infographic A visual image that is used to represent information or data.

metacognition The ability to reflect on your own work and the progress you've made through experience, choices, and mistakes.

multimedia Using more than one medium of expression or communication.

navigable Easy to get around in or maneuver around.

pitch A succinct description of your personal and professional goals.

platform A system that can be programmed and customized by outside users.

résumé A brief list of one's education, qualifications, and past experience.

syllabus An outline of the subjects in a course of study, major, or minor.

template A preset format for a document or file so that the format does not have to be re-created each time it is used.

ubiquitous Commonplace, present, or found everywhere.

URL (uniform resource locator) A protocol for specifying addresses on the internet.

FOR MORE INFORMATION

ACM SIGGRAPH: Association for Computing Machinery's Special Interest Group on Graphics and Interactive Techniques
2 Penn Plaza, Suite 701
New York, NY 10121
(800) 342-6626
Website: http://www.siggraph.org
This worldwide organization is a special interest group of the Association for Computing Machinery and is open to college students.

American Society for Engineering Education (ASEE)
1818 N Street NW, Suite 600
Washington, DC 20036
(202) 331-3500
Website: http://www.asee.org
This organization provides technology education and career resources for students in grades K–12, including a student newsletter, magazine, blog, and career center.

Association of Information Technology Professionals (AITP)
401 North Michigan Avenue, Suite 2400
Chicago, IL 60611
(800) 224-9371
Website: http://www.aitp.org
This is a society of professionals in information technology that has chapters for college students.

Entertainment Software Association of Canada
130 Spadina Avenue, Suite 408

Toronto, ON M5V 2L4
Canada
(416) 620-7171
Website: http://www.theesa.ca
This organization provides reports on topics such as the state of
the computer game industry in Canada, as well as news related
to entertainment software.

Information Technology Association of Canada
5090 Explorer Drive, Suite 801
Mississauga, ON L4W 4T9
Canada
(905) 602-8345
Website: http://www.itac.ca
This organization sponsors various forums on IT topics, publishes
research reports on several aspects of the IT industry in Canada,
and provides the latest news on its website.

National Association of Colleges and Employers (NACE)
62 Highland Avenue
Bethlehem, PA 18017
(610) 868-1421
Website: http://www.naceweb.org
This organization connects college career service professionals
nationwide, as well as university relations, recruiting professionals, and business affiliates to provide information on em-
ployment trends and the job market.

Software and Information Industry Association (SIIA)
1090 Vermont Avenue NW, 6th Floor
Washington, DC 20005
(202) 289-7442

Website: http://www.siia.net

This organization offers a variety of daily and weekly newsletters on the software industry, informational meetings, and webcasts.

WEBSITES

Because of the changing nature of internet links, Rosen Publishing has developed an online list of websites related to the subject of this book. This site is updated regularly. Please use this link to access the list:

http://www.rosenlinks.com/PROJL/apply

FOR FURTHER READING

Bennett, Ruth. *Tips for Better Social Networking*. New York, NY: Gareth Stevens, 2014.

Clazie, Ian. *Creating Your Digital Portfolio*. New York, NY: F+W Media, 2010.

Endsley, Kezia. *Website Design*. New York, NY: Cavendish Square, 2015.

Henneberg, Susan. *Effective Job Hunting and Career Preparedness*. New York, NY: Rosen Publishing, 2015.

Light, Tracy Penny, et al. *Documenting Learning with ePortfolios*. Hoboken, NJ: Wiley, 2011.

Marzoff, Julie. *Online Privacy*. New York, NY: Gareth Stevens, 2013.

Poolos, J. *Designing, Building, and Maintaining Web Sites*. New York, NY: Rosen, 2011.

Small, Cathleen. *Make the Most of Tumblr and Other Blogging Platforms*. New York, NY: Cavendish Square, 2015.

Spilsbury, Louise. *Tips for Better Writing*. New York, NY: Gareth Stevens, 2014.

Willett, Edward. *Career Building Through Using Digital Design Tools*. New York, NY: Rosen Publishing, 2014.

BIBLIOGRAPHY

Anderson, Denise. *Stand Out: Design a Personal Brand. Build a Killer Portfolio. Find a Great Design Job.* Berkeley, CA: Peachpit Press, 2016.

Baron, Cynthia L. *Designing a Digital Portfolio: Edition 2.* Berkeley, CA: New Riders, 2010.

Chisolm, Alison Cooper, and Anna Ivey. *How to Prepare a Standout College Application: Expert Advice that Takes You from LMO* (Like Many Others) to Admit.* San Francisco, CA: Jossey-Bass, 2013.

The Creative Group. "Digital Portfolio Review: Find the Best, Filter Through the Rest." Robert Half, May 12, 2016. https://www.roberthalf.com/creativegroup/blog/digital-portfolio -review-find-the-best-filter-through-the-rest.

DeCarlo, Laura. *Résumés For Dummies.* Hoboken, NJ: Wiley, 2015.

Hicks, Kristen. "5 Free Tools For Making Digital Portfolios." Edudemic, February 9, 2015. http://www.edudemic.com /tools-for-digital-portfolios.

Hiles, Heather. "Goodbye Résumés, Hello Digital Portfolios." Getting Smart, April 23, 2016. http://gettingsmart.com /2016/04/goodbye-resumes-hello-digital-portfolios-2.

Kelsey, Todd. *Getting Started with WordPress: Design Your Own Blog or Website.* Australia: Course Technology PTR/Cengage Learning, 2012.

Miller, Ross, and Wende Morgaine. "The Benefit of E-portfolios for Students and Faculty in Their Own Words." AACU. Accessed October 15, 2016. https://www.aacu.org /publications-research/periodicals/benefits-e-portfolios -students-and-faculty-their-own-words.

Morgan, Hannah. *The Infographic Résumés: How to Create a Visual Portfolio that Showcases Your Skills and Lands the Job.* New York, NY: McGraw-Hill Education, 2014.

Myers, Debbie Rose. *The Graphic Designer's Guide to Portfolio Design.* Hoboken, NJ: Wiley & Sons, 2009.

Salpeter, Miriam. *Social Networking for Career Success: Using Online Tools to Create a Personal Brand.* New York, NY: LearningExpress, 2011.

Vander Ark, Tom. "Every Student Should Have a Digital Portfolio." Huffington Post, June 24, 2016. http://www .huffingtonpost.com/tom-vander-ark/every-student-should -have_b_7649914.html.

Volk, Larry, and Danielle Currier. *No Plastic Sleeves.* New York, NY: Focal Press, 2015.

Washington and Lee University. "How to Create a Digital Portfolio."Accessed October 2, 2016. https://www.wlu.edu /career-development/students/professional-online-presence /digital-portfolios-and-professional-websites/how-to-create -a-digital-portfolio.

Westervelt, Eric. "The Big New Effort to Revamp College Admissions—Will It Work?" NPR, September 30, 2015. http://www.npr.org/sections/ed/2015/09/30/444498625 /the-big-new-effort-to-revamp-college-admissions-will-it -work.

INDEX

ABOUT THE AUTHOR

Natalie Chomet is a marketer of children's and young adult educational books and digital resources. Chomet has experience creating and editing digital content such as websites, emails, and more. She enjoys reading, editing, and writing short stories in her spare time. Chomet currently resides in Brooklyn, New York.

PHOTO CREDITS